LITHUANIA

LITHUANIA

THEN & NOW

Prepared by
Geography Department

Lerner Publications Company
Minneapolis

Series editors: Mary M. Rodgers, Tom Streissguth,
   Colleen Sexton
Photo researcher: Bill Kauffmann
Designer: Zachary Marell

Our thanks to the following people for their help in
preparing and checking the text of this book: Dr. Craig
ZumBrunnen, Department of Geography, University of
Washington; Karen Sirvaitis; and Diana B. Vidutis,
Embassy of Lithuania, Washington, D.C.

Pronunciation Guide

Gediminas	ged-ih-MIN-ahs
glasnost	GLAZ-nost
Klaipėda	KLY-pehd-eh
Kuršiu Marios	COOR-shoo MAH-ree-os
Drūkšiai	DROOK-shay
perestroika	pehr-eh-STROY-kah
Sajudis	SAH-yoo-diss

Words in **bold** type are listed in a glossary that starts on page 52.

LIBRARY OF CONGRESS CATALOGING-IN-PUBLICATION DATA

Lithuania / prepared by Geography Department, Lerner Publica-
   tions Company.
       p.   cm. — (Then & now)
   Includes index.
   Summary: Discusses Lithuania's geography, ethnic mixture,
history, political events, economic activities, environmental
hazards, relations with neighbors, and future.
   ISBN 0–8225–2804–5 (lib. bdg.)
   1. Lithuania—History—Juvenile literature. [1. Lithuania.]
I. Lerner Publications Company. Geography Dept. II. Series:
Then & Now (Minneapolis, Minn.)
DK505.56.L58 1992
947'.5—dc20   92–9698
                                                        CIP
                                                        AC

Manufactured in the United States of America

2 3 4 5 6 – I/JR – 98 97 96 95 94 93

At Gediminas Square in Vilnius, the capital of Lithuania, shoppers visit beneath a religious statue that is part of Vilnius Cathedral.

"What was stolen must be returned."

Vytautas Landsbergis
January 14, 1990

In 1992, the Soviet Union would have celebrated the 75th anniversary of the revolution of 1917. During that revolt, political activists called **Communists** overthrew the czar (ruler) and the government of the **Russian Empire**. The revolution of 1917 was the first step in establishing the 15-member **Union of Soviet Socialist Republics (USSR).**

The Soviet Union stretched from eastern Europe across northern Asia and contained nearly 300 million people. Within this vast nation, the Communist government guaranteed housing, education, health care, and lifetime employment. Communist leaders told farmers and factory workers that Soviet citizens owned all property in common. The new nation quickly **industrialized**, meaning it built many new factories and upgraded existing ones. It also modernized and enlarged its farms. In addition, the USSR created a huge, well-equipped military force that allowed it to become one of the most powerful nations in the world.

In 1989, hundreds of thousands of people from the Baltic countries of Lithuania, Latvia, and Estonia linked hands and arms to form a human chain. It stretched from Vilnius through Riga in Latvia to Tallinn in Estonia—a distance of nearly 400 miles (644 kilometers). The event protested the Soviet takeover of the Baltics in 1940.

By the early 1990s, the Soviet Union was in a period of rapid change and turmoil. The central government had mismanaged the economy, which was failing to provide goods. To control the various ethnic groups within the USSR, the Communists had long restricted many freedoms. People throughout the vast nation were dissatisfied.

These Lithuanian elementary students attend classes in a building that is more than 500 years old.

In a forested park, hikers trek amid trees that are taking on the colors of autumn.

Since reestablishing their nation's independence in 1991, Lithuanians often display the country's yellow, green, and red flag.

Lithuania—a small republic in north central Europe that the Soviets had occupied since 1940—declared its independence from the USSR in March 1990. The Soviet president, Mikhail Gorbachev, denied this claim. To pressure the Lithuanians into staying in the union, he cut off supplies of oil and other raw materials and sent tanks to Vilnius, the capital of Lithuania. Despite these actions, Lithuanians continued their struggle for self-rule. In January 1991, a confrontation between pro-independence activists and Soviet troops ended in bloodshed. The violence made Lithuanians even more determined to end Soviet rule of their territory.

At the same time, other Soviet republics were also claiming independence—a development that worried some old-style Communist leaders. In August 1991, these conservative Communists tried to use Soviet military power to overthrow the Soviet president. Their effort failed and hastened the breakup of the USSR.

Soon after the revolt against Gorbachev collapsed, the Lithuanian parliament again declared Lithuania free of Soviet rule. This time, neither Gorbachev nor Soviet tanks could prevent Lithuanian independence from becoming a reality.

Many of the former Soviet republics formed the **Commonwealth of Independent States (CIS)**, a loose federation. Lithuanians chose not to join the CIS, but in September 1991, the **United Nations** welcomed Lithuania into its ranks as a free, self-governing country.

CHAPTER ONE

The Land and People of Lithuania

U ntil recently, many people would have had difficulty finding Lithuania on a map. Located in the northwestern corner of the old USSR, Lithuania was often labeled as Russia, the largest and most powerful former Soviet republic. But the dramatic events of the early 1990s have sparked widespread interest in the newly independent Republic of Lithuania.

• The Lay of the Land •

With 25,174 square miles (65,201 square kilometers) of territory, Lithuania is slightly bigger than the state of West Virginia and is slightly smaller than Scotland. Lithuania, however, is the largest of the three independent republics that lie along the Baltic Sea. These nations—Lithuania, Latvia, and Estonia —together are known as the **Baltic States.**

Friends wait outside the modern-style Palace of Weddings in Vilnius for newlyweds to make their first public appearance.

Sand dunes mixed with shrubs and grasses are features of the Ne-ringa Peninsula—a narrow strip of land that juts into the Baltic Sea.

Latvia is Lithuania's northern neighbor. To the southeast lies Belarus, another former Soviet republic. To the southwest are Poland and Kaliningrad, a small Russian territory that is surrounded by Lithuania, Poland, and the Baltic Sea. An arm of the North Atlantic Ocean, the Baltic forms the 62-mile (100-km) shoreline of western Lithuania.

Sand dunes and pine forests line Lithuania's Baltic coast. A narrow strip of land called the Neringa Peninsula lies offshore, separating Kuršiu Marios—a large, fish-filled lagoon—from the Baltic Sea. In recent decades, heavy industrialization has polluted the lagoon.

The country's flat inland terrain never exceeds 1,000 feet (305 meters) above sea level. Low-lying plains and gently sloping uplands—both part of the East European Plain—dominate the landscape. Woodlands, mostly of evergreen trees, cover about one-fourth of Lithuania. Although only half of the country's soil is fertile, Lithuania has some of the

Hand-carved wooden sculptures that depict Christian religious figures dot the byways of the Lithuanian countryside.

Taking advantage of Lithuania's fertile soil, homeowners plant and harvest food in small plots near their dwellings.

most productive farmland in north central Europe. Lakes and wetlands (swampy areas) make up large sections of the country that are not farmed.

Lithuania has more than 800 rivers. The republic's longest waterways are the Nemunas, the Neris, and the Venta, all of which eventually empty into the Baltic Sea. Nearly 80 percent of the nation's 3,000 lakes and reservoirs are located in the scenic uplands of eastern Lithuania. Lakes Drūkšiai and Dysnai are the largest, and Lake Tauragnas is the deepest. The Kaunas Reservoir, another large inland body of water, lies southeast of the city of Kaunas.

A family picks wild blueberries in a forested section of southern Lithuania.

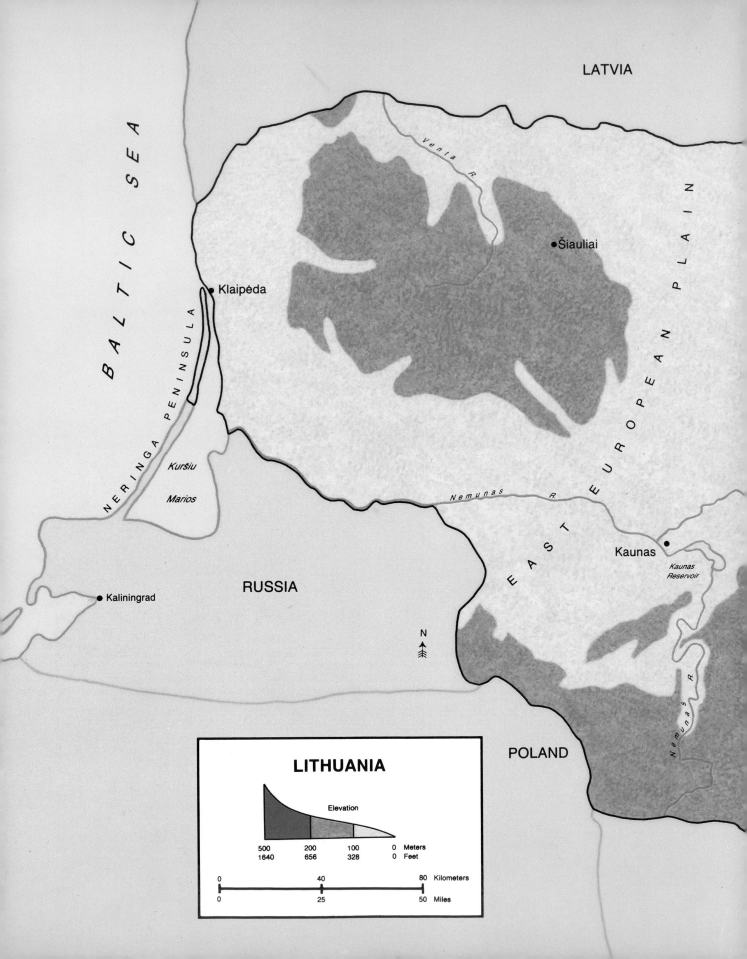

LATVIA

BALTIC SEA

Venta R.

●Šiauliai

●Klaipėda

NERINGA PENINSULA

Kuršiu

Marios

Nemunas R.

EAST EUROPEAN PLAIN

Kaunas ●

Kaunas Reservoir

RUSSIA

● Kaliningrad

N

Nemunas R.

POLAND

LITHUANIA

Elevation

| 500 | 200 | 100 | 0 | Meters |
| 1640 | 656 | 328 | 0 | Feet |

0   40   80 Kilometers

0   25   50 Miles

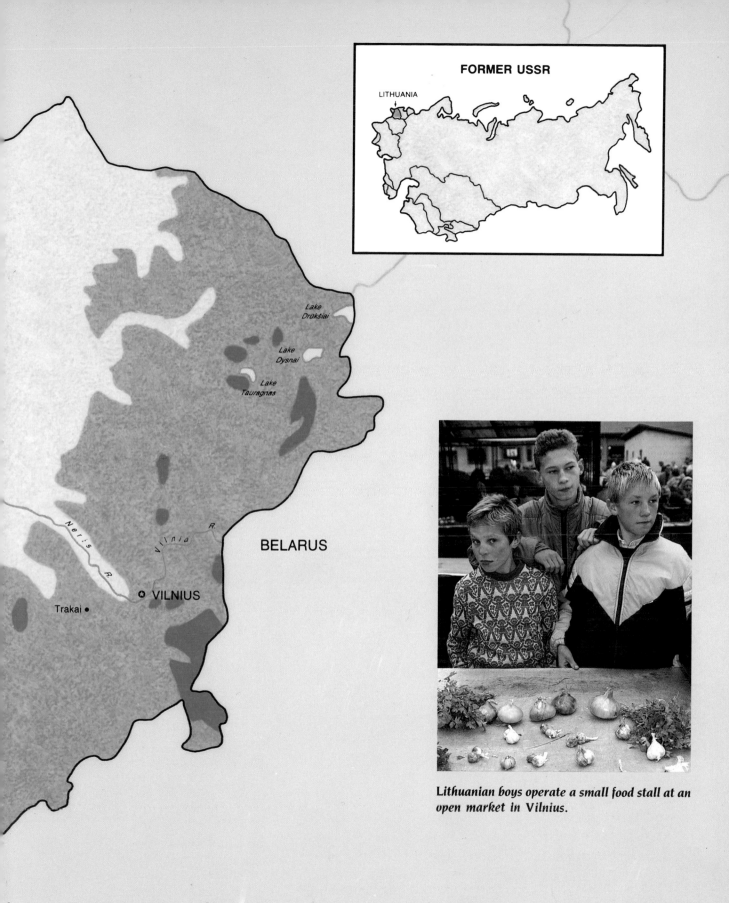

FORMER USSR

LITHUANIA

Lake
Drūkšiai

Lake
Dysnai

Lake
Tauragnas

Neris R.

Vilnia R.

BELARUS

⊛ VILNIUS

Trakai •

**Lithuanian boys operate a small food stall at an
open market in Vilnius.**

• *Climate* •

For a northern country, Lithuania has a fairly moderate climate. Strong winds blow in from the North Atlantic Ocean and bring mild temperatures to areas along the Baltic Sea. Winter readings are highest near the coast, where they average 27°F (−3°C). Winter temperatures drop to about 21°F (−6°C) in eastern Lithuania. Coastal and inland weather varies little during the summer, when average temperatures throughout the country hover around 60°F (16°C).

Annual rainfall along the coasts and in the highlands east of Vilnius exceeds 32 inches (80 centimeters). The rest of the country receives between 24 inches (60 cm) and 32 inches (80 cm) per year. Rainfall accounts for 75 percent of Lithuania's precipitation. The rest comes in the form of snow.

Because Lithuania lies in the northern part of the Northern Hemisphere, the country experiences a summer change called the **midnight sun.** During June, July, and August, when the northern half of the world is tilted toward the sun, Lithuania has as many as 18 hours of daylight and very short nights. On the other hand, in winter, when the same area is angled away from the sun, Lithuanians experience equally long nights and very brief days.

• *Cities* •

Lithuania's three largest urban centers—Vilnius, Kaunas, and Klaipėda—were founded many centuries ago. They contain a blend of architectural styles that reflect the country's ancient origins as well as its modern economic activities.

Vilnius (population 593,000) is the country's capital and main industrial hub. According to legend, Gediminas, the grand duke of Lithuania in the 1300s, was told in a dream to build his capital

Autumn weather in Lithuania is cold enough for children to wear thick jackets and woolen hats.

on a pair of hills where Vilnius now stands. Founded where the Neris and Vilnia rivers meet in southeastern Lithuania, the city became Lithuania's first permanent capital in 1323.

Old Town, the ancient section of Vilnius, is known for the quaint buildings that line its narrow, cobblestone streets. In previous centuries, Gediminas Square held a farmers' market. More recently, it has been the site of historic public gatherings in Lithuania's struggle for independence. Modern buildings —such as the Opera and Ballet Theater and the Palace of Weddings—give Vilnius an up-to-date look.

Population increases during the 20th century have burdened Vilnius with a severe housing shortage. To meet the rising demand for shelter, the government is constructing new apartment complexes in and around the city.

Kaunas (population 430,000) is located in central Lithuania at the junction of the Nemunas and Neris rivers. The Lithuanian leader Kaunas, who

The view of Vilnius from the tower in Gediminas Square shows the capital's many administrative buildings and public gardens.

In the oldest parts of Kaunas, the nation's industrial metropolis in central Lithuania, workers have restored buildings and churches that date from the city's early days as a trading hub.

built a castle here, established the city as a trading center in the 11th century. In addition to the castle's ruins, Kaunas also has old churches, monasteries, and squares. Still a commercial crossroads, the city is connected to many other large hubs in the region by rivers, railroads, and highways.

Klaipėda, on the Baltic Sea at the mouth of the Nemunas River, is Lithuania's only port. Many of the city's 200,000 people depend on the sea for their livelihood by fishing, building ships, or working in fish-processing plants.

Founded as a fort in the mid-1200s, Klaipėda later became an important town within the Hanseatic League, an ancient trading organization in northern Europe. Ships from many foreign countries call at Klaipėda's harbor, which provides Lithuania with a vital link to north central Europe. Lithuania earns income by charging tolls for the use of Klaipėda's port facilities.

In the age-old seaport of Klaipėda, a huge trawler sits in a floating dock. Once known as Memel, Klaipėda has a multinational past, having been held at times between the 12th and 20th centuries by Germany, Sweden, and Russia. The port remains a major shipbuilding center.

Folk groups perform traditional Lithuanian music in a street in downtown Vilnius.

Two elderly Lithuanians exchange views on a park bench.

• Ethnic Heritage and Language •

Unlike Latvia and Estonia—where heavy immigration from Russia and other Soviet republics occurred between 1940 and 1990—Lithuania has had a stable ethnic mixture. Fewer Russians emigrated to Lithuania because the country is less industrialized than the other Baltic States. **Ethnic Russians** tended to go where factory skills were most in demand. About 80 percent of Lithuania's 3.7 million people are **ethnic Lithuanians.** Ethnic Russians make up 9 percent of the population, followed by smaller numbers of Poles, Belarussians, Ukrainians, and Jews.

Since Lithuania restored its independence in 1990, its ethnic minorities, particularly Russians, have feared the loss of their civil rights. These worries prompted Lithuania and Russia to sign a treaty guaranteeing the rights of Russians in Lithuania and of Lithuanians in Russia. Yet, most Russians living in Lithuania wish to remain there and voted for independence.

A *young reader enjoys vividly illustrated children's books at a school library in Trakai, southeastern Lithuania.*

In a restored synagogue (Jewish house of worship) in Vilnius, a blue curtain guards the entrance to the ark—a chest that holds scrolls of the Torah (scriptures). In earlier times, many Jews lived in the capital. During World War II (1939–1945), however, the German army occupied Lithuania and killed thousands of Jews in Vilnius.

Lithuanian, which falls within the Baltic branch of Indo-European tongues, replaced Russian as the country's official language in 1990. Many Lithuanians speak Russian, but few Russians in Lithuania can communicate in the Lithuanian language.

Lithuanian is similar to Latvian—the only other living Baltic language. Citizens of Lithuania and Latvia are not able to understand one another, even though their languages are both written in the Latin alphabet. The Cyrillic alphabet is used to write Russian and other Slavic languages.

• Religion and Festivals •

European missionaries and soldiers spent several hundred years trying to establish the Roman Catholic faith in Lithuania, where the people supported religions that honored the forces of nature. By the late 1300s, Lithuania's leaders had accepted

Christianity, which eventually became the faith of the people as well. Roughly 80 percent of Lithuanians who profess religious beliefs follow Roman Catholicism. Protestants, Russian Orthodox believers, and Jews make up most of the remaining 20 percent.

During the 50 years of Soviet rule, the central government severely limited religious gatherings. Believers were often denied access to higher education. Some lost their jobs or were sent to prison. Many churches fell into disrepair or were used as museums or warehouses. Workers are now renovating churches and synagogues throughout the country, and Lithuanians are again openly celebrating religious services and holidays without fear of persecution.

In addition to religious occasions, Lithuanians also hold nonreligious festivals that are often highlighted by choral singing. During these festivals, costumed dancers and musicians perform ancient steps and folk songs before thousands of spectators. Every five years, Vingis Park in Vilnius is the site of a folk music festival. The park contains a concert stage that can accommodate 20,000 performers.

A Roman Catholic (above) *prays at an outdoor religious shrine in Vilnius. Under Soviet rule, the Catholic religion — which most Lithuanians follow — was severely restricted. Many people continued to express their faith at the Hill of Crosses* (right)*, which lies near the northern city of Šiauliai. Devout Catholics positioned the crosses, which Soviet authorities tore down or burned, only to have the faithful return and rebuild the display. The most recent attempt to level the shrine was in 1975, and since then the number of crosses has multiplied into the thousands. Tradition dictates that every visitor to the hill leave a cross.*

• *Education* •

More than 60 percent of Lithuania's children go to some form of preschool. From age 6 to 17, students attend one of the country's 2,200 primary and secondary schools. The University of Vilnius, the oldest institution of higher learning in the old USSR, dates to 1579. Lithuania also has many other post-secondary schools that offer technical training.

Since independence, Lithuanian educators have begun to reform courses and teaching methods to eliminate studies that were imposed under Soviet rule. For example, classes in military preparation and Communist ideology are being replaced by classes in psychology and sociology. Teachers also are easing the strict methods that the Soviets required them to use.

During the 50 years of Soviet rule, most classes in Lithuania were taught in the Lithuanian language. Russian and Polish students also could learn in their native tongues. Classes continue to be offered in all three languages, but anyone who now wants to function in Lithuanian society needs a good command of written and spoken Lithuanian.

• *Health Care* •

Under Soviet leadership, the government paid for all health care in Lithuania. Patients sometimes received inadequate treatment, however, because medicines often were not available and hospitals

Classmates chat under an arcade at the University of Vilnius. Stephen Báthory – a Hungarian king of the Polish-Lithuanian Commonwealth – founded the school as a Jesuit academy in 1579.

were understaffed. The Lithuanian government is now developing a new health plan that may use national funds to invest in improved equipment and more medicines.

Hundreds of hospitals and clinics continue to operate throughout Lithuania, although much of the medical equipment is still outdated. After independence, foreign health-care specialists arrived to train Lithuanian doctors and nurses in the latest medical technologies.

Cancer is among the leading causes of death in Lithuania, and alcoholism is a common problem. Yet the average life expectancy of a Lithuanian born today is 72, which compares well with former Soviet republics and with eastern European states.

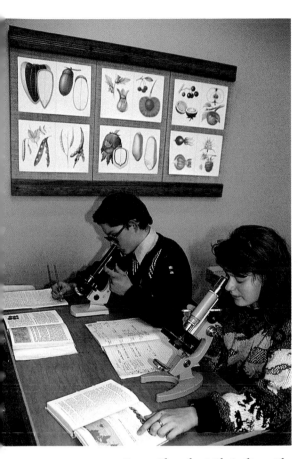

Beneath a chart that shows the growth of plants, 14-year-old Lithuanian students use microscopes to analyze seeds in a botany class.

A doctor and nurse examine a patient at a state-run hospital in Vilnius. With the help of foreign investors, educators, and technicians, Lithuania's health-care system is undergoing reorganization and modernization.

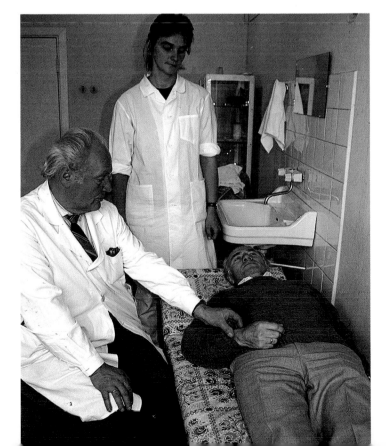

CHAPTER TWO

Lithuania's Story

L ithuanians are among the most ancient peoples of Europe. Legends say they are descended from the Romans, but it is more likely that they arrived from Asia at least 4,000 years ago and perhaps as long as 10,000 years ago. In fact, some language scholars believe Lithuanian is related to the Sanskrit language of ancient India.

Early Lithuanians worshiped gods who were believed to control natural forces, such as thunder and fire. Most families farmed the land or hunted and gathered their food. In time, groups of families formed strong, self-governing communities. The dukes of Lithuania—who were wealthy and powerful landowners—later united these groups and offered them protection from foreign invasions.

The dukedoms in the area banded together in the early 13th century to form the grand dukedom of Lithuania. They hoped that by combining their forces they could counter the actions of the **Order**

Trakai Castle, built on a small island within a lake, was once the stronghold of the grand dukes of Lithuania, who ruled the region from the 13th through the 15th centuries.

A member of the religious Order of Teutonic Knights is shown holding the group's red-and-white shield. The knights spent centuries trying to convert the Lithuanian people to Christianity by force. During these efforts, the invaders annexed (took over) land from some Lithuanians who would not accept the new faith.

of Teutonic Knights. This German religious-military organization was attacking the Baltic region in the name of the Roman Catholic pope (leader), who sent the knights to convert the Lithuanians to Christianity.

• Grand Dukes of Lithuania •

In 1236, the dukes of Lithuania elected Mindaugas as their first grand duke. He successfully fought against the Teutonic knights for 20 years. He also triumphed against the Tatars, a central Asian people who had invaded much of eastern Europe during the early 13th century.

In the early 14th century, Gediminas became grand duke. The new leader's main concern was the ongoing threat of the Teutonic knights, who were still trying to force the Lithuanians to accept Christianity. To strengthen his position in the region, Gediminas arranged the marriage of his daughter Aldona to Prince Casimir of Poland. At this time, Poland was a strong Catholic realm. Through this alliance, the grand duke hoped to spare the Lithuanians from further Teutonic attacks.

When not at war, Gediminas set about improving his dukedom, whose capital was at Trakai in the southeastern part of the country. Gediminas founded Vilnius near Trakai and built up Kaunas as an important center of trade. Merchants from all over Europe sailed up the Nemunas River to Kaunas to buy **amber**, honey, and furs. In 1323, Gediminas moved Lithuania's seat of government from Trakai to Vilnius.

• *Christianity and Vytautas* •

In 1385, Gediminas's grandson Jogaila became grand duke of Lithuania. In the same year, Jogaila agreed to marry Poland's Queen Jadwiga, a devout Roman Catholic. The marriage pact, called the Krevo Union, required Jogaila to convert from traditional beliefs to Catholicism. Jogaila was baptized and married in 1386. He became the king of Poland and took the name Wladyslaw II Jagiello but also remained grand duke of Lithuania as Jogaila. One of his first acts was to officially decree Lithuania a Christian nation—the last European country to accept the faith.

Grand Duke Gediminas ably ruled Lithuania from 1316 to 1341. He founded Vilnius, where he built a large castle that still stands. Although he was repeatedly offered baptism into the Christian faith, Gediminas refused and continued to fight the Teutonic knights. To strengthen his position in the region, Gediminas arranged for his daughter to marry a Polish prince. This alliance later resulted in Lithuania's conversion to Christianity through another marriage pact between a Roman Catholic Polish queen and a Lithuanian grand duke.

Despite this change, most Lithuanians continued to follow their traditional religious beliefs. They rallied around Jogaila's cousin Vytautas, who had helped Jogaila to fight the Teutonic knights. Conflict between Jogaila and Vytautas seemed likely. To avoid it, Jogaila named Vytautas regent (royal trustee) of the grand dukedom in 1392. Meanwhile, Jogaila continued to reign over Poland.

Vytautas, who was the only Lithuanian leader to be dubbed "the Great," began a golden age in Lithuania. He expanded his country's borders from the Baltic Sea southward to the Black Sea and from Poland eastward nearly to Moscow, a large city in Russia. During Vytautas's reign, Lithuania's military

A knowledgeable diplomat and skilled commander, Vytautas the Great ushered in an era of cultural, economic, and religious growth in Lithuania during the 14th and 15th centuries.

Coins from the time of Vytautas show the national emblem of Lithuania (top) **and the columns of Gediminas's castle in Vilnius** (bottom).

In 1410, *a combined force of Lithuanians and Poles thrashed the Teutonic knights at the Battle of Tannenberg (a town in Poland).*

strength was unmatched in eastern Europe. In 1410, for example, Lithuanian and Polish soldiers won the Battle of Tannenberg, which finally drove the Teutonic knights from the region. The dukedom's powerful army also prevented the Tatars, who held much of eastern Europe, from reaching western Europe.

In the early 1400s, Lithuania was about four times bigger than Poland and included the lands of modern Ukraine and Belarus. An agreement that Jogaila and Vytautas had made allowed Poland to absorb Lithuania upon Vytautas's death in 1430. Lithuanian nobles then prepared to elect a new grand duke, whose appointment now required Poland's approval.

• *Russian Wars and Partitions* •

In the 15th century, frequent disagreements marred the alliance between Poland and Lithuania. Many of Vytautas's successors proved to be poor leaders who weakened the dukedom's government. In addition, the duchy (dukedom) of Moscow was extending its territory westward toward Lithuania. Throughout the 1400s, Moscow's forces seized Lithuanian lands and put them under the control of Muscovite princes.

Lithuania eventually turned to Poland for assistance against Moscow. In exchange for military aid, Poland demanded a more permanent union with Lithuania. Although most Lithuanians wanted to remain independent of Poland, their leaders knew that Lithuania was not strong enough to fend off the Russians. As a result, Lithuania agreed to unite with Poland. The unification ceremony took place in Lublin, Poland, in 1569.

The Union of Lublin created the Polish-Lithuanian Commonwealth, a new state with its capital in Kraków, Poland. Each nation kept its local administrations and armies, but Lithuania lost much of its national authority and identity. In fact, while it was a part of the commonwealth, Lithuania was often referred to as Poland.

Under the Union of Lublin, members of the Lithuanian and Polish nobilities elected the head of the commonwealth. To find someone neutral, the nobles often chose a leader from a foreign nation to be king. From 1573 to 1733, the union's kings came from countries such as France, Hungary, Sweden, and Germany. Many of these rulers cared little about the culture of either Lithuania or Poland.

During the 1700s, the increasingly powerful forces of Russia stepped up their attacks on Lithuania. The constant warfare caused famines that killed thousands of Lithuanians. By 1772, the Polish-

Partition of 1793

Russian Partitions (late 1700s)

- Polish-Lithuanian Commonwealth
- To Prussia
- To Russia
- To Austria
- Current border of Lithuania

Partition of 1772

Partition of 1795

Miles
0 50 100 200

0 100 200
Kilometers

Lithuanian Commonwealth was so weak that Russia was able to enforce the First Partition (division), during which it seized the eastern provinces of Lithuania. These territories had been Lithuanian since the time of Gediminas. Prussia (now part of Germany) and Austria absorbed sections of Poland.

By 1793, after the Second Partition was completed, Russia had taken over the remaining eastern provinces of Lithuania. Within two years, however, Poland and Lithuania revolted against the Russians. The uprising failed, and Russia began the Third Partition in 1795, claiming most of the rest of Lithuania.

• Russification •

Lithuanians and Poles failed in revolts against Russian control in 1831 and 1863. In 1864, Alexander II, the czar of the Russian Empire, appointed Mikhail Muravyov governor-general of Lithuania. Alexander II ordered Muravyov to **Russify** Lithuania by forcibly introducing the Russian language, the Russian Orthodox religion, and Russian laws. These changes were meant to eliminate unrest by ending the cultural expressions of discontent.

Muravyov tried to destroy the influence of the Roman Catholic Church in Lithuania by restricting religious rituals. To force the acceptance of Russian, he also forbade the publication of anything in the Lithuanian alphabet. Many Lithuanian intellectuals, however, protested against this attack on their culture by continuing to write in Lithuanian. Those who took part in the underground movement were exiled or executed. Within a year of the governor-general's arrival, about 10,000 Lithuanians had lost either their freedom or their lives.

Not everyone in Lithuania participated in the movement. Under Russian rule, most Lithuanians continued to farm the land either on small plots or on large estates. Much of the harvest went to feed the growing population of the Russian Empire. The ice-free Baltic port of Klaipėda gave the empire the means to trade with the rest of Europe. These contacts drew Russia—as well as Lithuania—into European affairs.

The national emblem of Lithuania features a knight on horseback holding a raised sword. Used on money and banners since the 14th century, the emblem has become a modern symbol of independent Lithuania.

• Lithuania on Its Own •

In 1914, many nations in Europe—including Russia—were preparing for an international conflict. Russia allied itself with Britain and France to oppose German forces. When Germany invaded France in 1914, World War I broke out in both western and eastern Europe.

Antanas Smetona, Lithuania's first president, led the Nationalist party. In coalition with other parties, he ruled from 1918 to 1920. After several years of government by liberal parties, Nationalist army officers overthrew the liberals and returned Smetona to power. He dissolved the Lithuanian parliament in 1927 and by 1930 had banned all opposition political parties. Despite these restrictions, his regime also enacted important reforms regarding land use and landownership. After the Soviets invaded in 1940, Smetona fled to the United States.

The German army also invaded Lithuania in 1914 and had control of the country by 1915. Although they were under military occupation, Lithuanians saw the war as an opportunity to free themselves from Russian rule. In February 1918, while Germany still occupied their country, Lithuanians declared their independence and elected Antanas Smetona president. By the end of the year, Germany had lost the war.

Meanwhile, the Russian Empire was collapsing. The world war had drained the country of money and men. Revolutionaries called Communists promised to establish a new system in which Russian workers would have a better life. By 1919, the Communists had overthrown the czar's government and were setting up a new nation that later became the Union of Soviet Socialist Republics (USSR).

As Russia underwent these drastic changes, the small, newly independent Republic of Lithuania drew up a constitution. Lithuanians chose yellow, green, and red for the colors of their flag and designed an official seal. The national anthem praised "the land of heroes." The litas became the country's monetary unit. Smetona held power until 1920. In that year, the Communist government of Russia recognized the republic as an independent state.

Although they had gained their freedom, Lithuanians had trouble agreeing on administrative and political matters. The unstable governments that followed Smetona's prompted a military takeover in 1926. The conservative Lithuanians who led the movement returned Smetona to power. His second term in office saw the decline of some democratic practices but also the enactment of important reforms in landownership and land use. Smetona remained president of Lithuania until 1940, when conflicts in Europe again changed Lithuania's status.

• *World War II and Soviet Annexation* •

Germany, under its leader Adolf Hitler, was expanding its armed forces and **annexing** neighboring countries. At the same time, the Soviet ruler Joseph Stalin was seeking control of the Baltic States. In August 1939, Germany and Russia signed the **Molotov-Ribbentrop Pact,** in which the two countries promised not to invade one another. A secret part of the treaty allowed the Soviets to add the Baltic States to the USSR.

World War II officially began in September 1939, when Germany invaded Poland. In 1940, the USSR annexed Lithuania. In the summer of 1941, however, Germany broke its agreement with the USSR by attacking the Soviet Union. The Baltic States were among the first areas to be overrun by German forces.

The Germans, who occupied Lithuania from 1941 until 1944, sent 160,000 Lithuanians to their deaths in **concentration camps.** More than 130,000 of the victims were Lithuanian Jews, whom the Germans singled out for their religious beliefs and ethnic background. By 1944, however, military setbacks in Russia forced the Germans to retreat westward. This movement gave the Soviet Red Army an opportunity to return to Lithuania.

The prospect of reoccupation by Soviet forces terrified Lithuanians, some of whom fled their homeland. Despite a lack of weapons and money, thousands of Lithuanians fought the Soviets. Through **mass deportations**, the Soviet government forcibly sent most of its Lithuanian opponents to labor camps in remote areas of the USSR. Although bitter fighting continued to erupt, by the early 1950s Lithuania was under Soviet control.

During the occupation, Lithuania became part of the Communist economy. The Soviet state took over private property, including farms that were

Modern Lithuanians put flowers on the railway tracks of Vilnius to commemorate those who lost their freedom during the Soviet mass deportations. Beginning in the 1940s, trains carried thousands of Lithuanians to remote areas of the USSR.

Despite Soviet efforts to suppress Lithuanian culture, the language and traditions of the small Baltic country continued to flourish. Musical events—such as this folk group performing from Castle Hill in Vilnius—helped to keep alive Lithuania's national identity.

brought into the Soviet **collective-farm program.** Soviet schools taught children to believe in the ideals of Communism, including state ownership of all property and atheism (the doctrine that denies the existence of God). The government also outlawed political opposition and restricted personal freedoms.

• *Glasnost to Independence* •

For decades, Lithuanians lived under the strict laws of the central Soviet government in Moscow. The situation eased in the late 1980s, when the Soviet leader Mikhail Gorbachev introduced the policies of ***glasnost*** and ***perestroika.*** In Russian, glasnost means "openness" and allowed Lithuanians —as well as other people in the USSR—to speak out against their government without fear of being punished. Perestroika, or restructuring, encouraged citizens to take active roles in reforming the USSR's social, economic, and political systems.

In April 1990, Sajudis—a Lithuanian anti-Soviet movement—staged a pro-independence rally in the capital that attracted thousands of flag-waving citizens.

On February 7, 1990, the Lithuanian Communist party—which was dominated by ethnic Lithuanians—affirmed that the USSR's annexation of Lithuania was illegal. A week later, Sajudis—a peaceful, pro-independence movement—declared its intention to restore self-rule to Lithuania. Under public pressure, the Communist party agreed to hold open national elections on February 24, 1990. Vytautas Landsbergis of Sajudis won election as president. On March 11, 1990, the Lithuanian parliament, in which Sajudis delegates had a majority, voted to declare the country's full independence from Soviet rule.

In response, the central Soviet government sent a convoy of Soviet tanks to Vilnius and cut supplies of oil and consumer goods. To get around this **embargo** (stoppage), Lithuanians bartered meat and dairy products for fuel from Poland, Russia, Belarus, and Latvia.

The Soviet embargo hurt Lithuanian industry. At the same time, however, Gorbachev's decisions regarding Lithuania drew international criticism. By the end of June, Lithuania and Moscow had agreed to negotiate, and the embargo ended.

Lithuanians were still demanding independence, however. On January 13, 1991—which Lithuanians call Bloody Sunday—Soviet tanks seized television and radio stations in Vilnius. During the confrontation, 14 Lithuanians were killed.

The violence strengthened the resolve of Lithuanian activists who were demanding immediate

Since independence, many aspects of economic and political life in Lithuania have changed, but trips to the local food markets are still common. Prices, however, are as much as five times higher than they were under the strictly controlled Soviet pricing system.

In 1991, Lithuanians hung rosaries and other religious symbols around a memorial to the activists crushed by tanks on January 13 of that year.

independence. A group of Soviet officials saw the demand as a sign that Gorbachev's authority over the Soviet Union was slipping. In August 1991, to maintain central control of the USSR, these conservative Communists attempted a **coup d'état** (sudden overthrow) of the Soviet government in Moscow. In Lithuania, Soviet soldiers took over additional communications facilities. In a struggle outside the parliament building, one Lithuanian was killed. In Moscow, however, massive demonstrations showed Russia's strong opposition to the coup, which soon collapsed.

Within days of the coup's failure, Lithuania again affirmed its independence. It had the support of nations in western Europe and even of Russia, which was severing its own ties to the USSR. In September 1991, Lithuania was admitted to the United Nations. For Lithuanians, World War II had finally ended.

CHAPTER THREE

Making
a Living
in Lithuania

Many Lithuanians are happy but nervous about their country's future. Much of their concern results from having been part of the Communist system, which made Lithuania economically dependent on the central government. Soviet regimes distributed goods, raw materials, and fuel. They set prices and **quotas** for agricultural products and industrial output. The central government chose the sites for new manufacturing plants and collective farms. As a result, none of the Baltic States was able to be self-sufficient.

The failure of this centralized system has forced the Lithuanian government to dismantle and reorganize the country's entire economy. One of the first goals is to update industries that have a chance to survive and compete. In this way, Lithuania will soon have high-quality goods to trade for fuel and raw

A woman cleans and shines the windows of a building in Old Town —the ancient section of Vilnius.

materials, which are in short supply. In the mean-time, Lithuania will trade with some of the former Soviet republics, which still provide a major market for Lithuanian goods.

*Economic unity among the Baltic States may be one of the keys to their financial survival. Here, **Anatoliss Gorbunovs of Latvia** (left), **Arnold Rüütel of Estonia** (middle), **and Vytautas Landsbergis of Lithuania** (right) sign an accord that pledges their nations to economic and military cooperation.*

• Agriculture and Fishing •

Lithuania has always been able to feed its citizens. Nearly half of the nation's land is level and fertile enough for farming. Lithuanians consume only 60 percent of their agricultural output and export surplus food to other countries.

Dairying dominates Lithuanian farming and takes place in all parts of the country. The nation's cattle, sheep, pigs, and chickens provide enough meat, eggs, and milk for export. A substantial amount of crop farming also occurs. Farmers plant cereal grains —mainly wheat, barley, and oats—in western and central areas. The interior also provides potatoes,

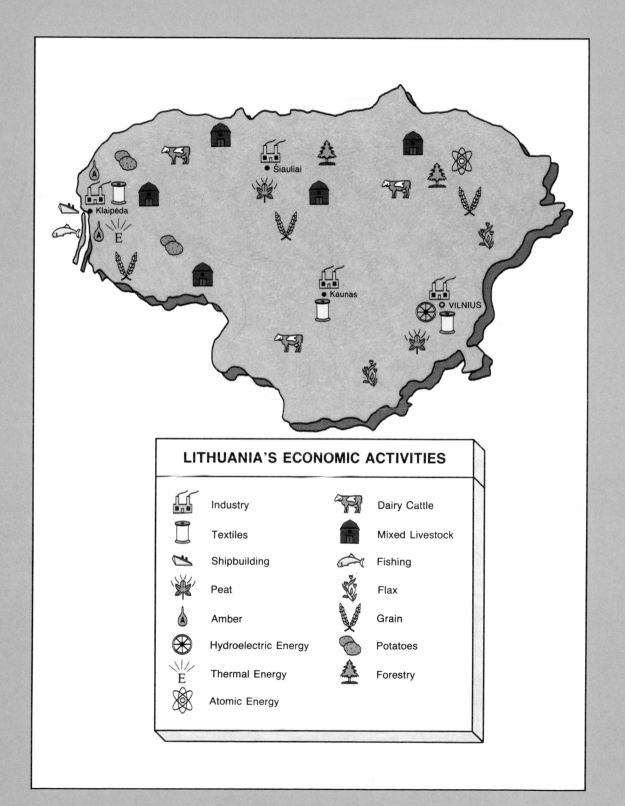

LITHUANIA'S ECONOMIC ACTIVITIES

Industry		Dairy Cattle	
Textiles		Mixed Livestock	
Shipbuilding		Fishing	
Peat		Flax	
Amber		Grain	
Hydroelectric Energy		Potatoes	
Thermal Energy		Forestry	
Atomic Energy			

a staple food, and sugar beets, which can be refined into sugar. Flax—a flowering herb whose fiber and seed are spun into cloth—is cultivated in eastern Lithuania.

The Lithuanian government is turning farms from state-run collectives into privately owned farms or into modern **cooperatives**, where workers own the land and work together to farm it. To increase output, private farmers will have to obtain up-to-date farm equipment and techniques. Since Lithuania's independence, foreign agricultural experts have been helping Lithuania to modernize its farming methods and machinery.

Another source of both food and income for Lithuanians is the nation's fishing industry. Roughly 98 percent of Lithuania's catch comes from fishing grounds in the Baltic Sea, in the Barents Sea north of Finland, and in the Atlantic Ocean. Trawlers—which drag nets along the seafloor—bring in herring, cod, and flounder. Fish farms use enclosed pens to raise carp and eel that supply Lithuania's inland lakes and ponds. Kuršiu Marios—a large, salty lagoon just south of Klaipėda—contains a variety of saltwater and freshwater fish.

Lying against a tall mound of ripening hay, a young Lithuanian (above) *enjoys the summer sunshine. Farmers* (below) *gather corn using modern harvesters.*

A bricklayer sets out his materials before beginning the job of placing and mortaring the clay blocks.

Workers at this factory in Vilnius assemble radios and televisions from imported parts.

• Manufacturing and Energy •

The Soviets built a few industries in Lithuania in the late 1940s. Because the country lacks raw materials, it specializes in making items from imported goods. Lithuania hopes to revive small industries —such as breweries, textile mills, and book binderies—that languished after the Soviets took over.

The factories of Kaunas, the nation's chief industrial hub, furnish machinery, construction materials, lumber, and farm equipment. Other Lithuanian plants refine oil, process chemicals, and produce consumer goods—including computers, television sets, and small household appliances. The country also makes furniture, paper, cement, textiles, and ships. Lithuania's high agricultural output has helped the growth of the food-processing industry.

Centuries ago, Lithuania's vast deposits of amber earned the country the nickname Amber Coast. A hardened tree resin found along the shores of the Baltic, amber still exists in great quantities in Lithuania. The yellow stone, worn in ancient times to ward off evil spirits, is used to make jewelry and other ornaments.

Nuclear Power in Lithuania

In 1986, the Chernobyl nuclear power plant in Ukraine exploded, and the resulting fire spewed poisonous substances into the air. Winds carried the toxic debris into Lithuania, which lies about 300 miles (483 km) northeast of Chernobyl. People and animals suffered burns, diseases, and other ailments from the fallout. This accident highlighted the dangers of northeastern Lithuania's Ignalina nuclear power plant, which is just like Chernobyl—only a lot bigger.

Lithuanian factories and cities depend on nuclear power stations to generate electricity. Nuclear plants create energy by splitting atoms of uranium—a **radioactive** chemical element. This energy is then converted into heat, which changes water in the facility to steam. The steam spins turbines that are attached to electrical generators.

The core, the main section of a nuclear power plant, is where the atom-splitting activity happens. Housed in a nuclear reactor, the core holds a set of fuel rods that contain the atoms of uranium. In most reactors, water is the moderator that comes in contact with the rods to create heat. A moderator regulates nuclear activity in a reactor.

In water-based reactors, if readings are not normal, the water stops circulating and nuclear operations cease. At plants like Ignalina, graphite—not water—is the moderator. When these reactors do not work properly, graphite and uranium continue to make heat, and large amounts of steam build up in the core. The pressure from the steam can cause

Several times in recent years, Lithuanian officials temporarily shut down the two nuclear reactors at the Ignalina plant (below) *because of fires. A diagram* (right) *shows how a nuclear facility in the United States might work. Unlike Ignalina, most U.S. facilities include a variety of safeguards, such as containment chambers, that lessen the chance of nuclear mishaps.*

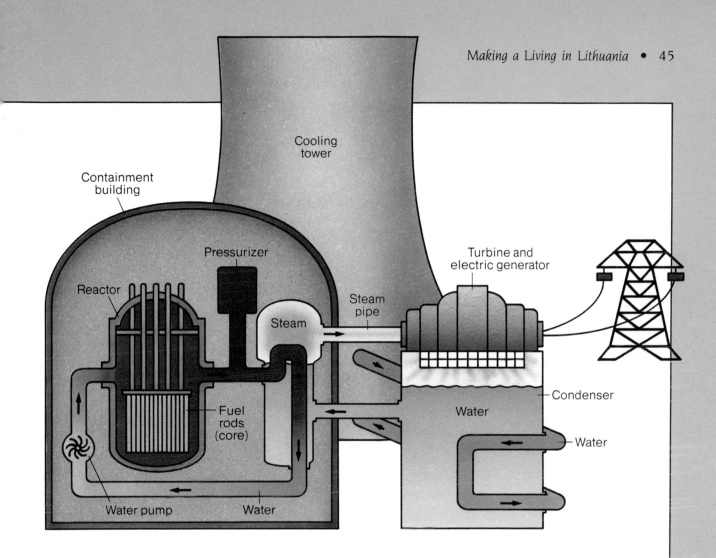

Containment building

Reactor

Pressurizer

Cooling tower

Steam

Steam pipe

Turbine and electric generator

Fuel rods (core)

Condenser

Water

Water

Water pump

Water

the nuclear generator to explode, and fires often result. This is what occurred at Chernobyl.

Another danger associated with nuclear energy is thermal pollution. The hottest parts of nuclear facilities are cooled with water. After it is used, the water—in thermal (heated) form—is usually released into a natural body of water. Water-based plants and animals often die when heated water is suddenly introduced into their habitat. Scientists believe that hot water from Ignalina has

harmed life in many lakes in northeastern Lithuania.

In 1988, inspectors shut down part of the Ignalina facility after a fire. In 1991, seven more stoppages occurred. Nuclear reactors in other countries are surrounded by protective containment chambers that can prevent harmful radioactive rays from escaping during accidents. Ignalina's reactor does not have this protection. For all of these reasons, Lithuanians are skeptical about the future of nuclear power in their country.

Modern computers help Lithuanian technicians to monitor the nuclear power plant at Ignalina. The scarcity of replacement equipment, however, hampers the workers' ability to keep the facility safe from accidents.

An economic obstacle to the success of large-scale industries is Lithuania's shortage of fossil fuels (coal and oil) and other energy sources. The country has small amounts of **peat** that meet some domestic fuel needs. The large Ignalina nuclear power plant in northeastern Lithuania produces energy for industry. Many people are concerned about the safety of this facility, which is a larger model of the Chernobyl plant that blew up in 1986. As a result, the future of nuclear energy in Lithuania is uncertain.

Under Soviet rule, Lithuania received low-cost fuel from Russia, which has vast deposits of oil, coal, and natural gas. In return, Russia got meat and dairy products from Lithuania at reduced prices. To fund its own economic recovery, Russia has raised its oil prices to approach global levels. To offset these costs, Lithuania charges Russia higher prices for food exports.

• Trade and Currency •

Trade with other nations is one of the keys to Lithuania's future financial success. The country will have a difficult time selling its manufactured goods at world-market prices, however, because many of its products are out of date or poorly made.

The Scandinavian countries in the Baltic region —Sweden, Norway, Denmark, and Finland—are bringing in funds to upgrade Lithuania's industries. In addition, some Scandinavian nations are setting up **joint ventures**—businesses sited in the Baltics that have a foreign partner as a major investor. If these actions make it possible for Lithuania, Latvia, and Estonia to buy and produce goods, all of the countries surrounding the Baltic Sea will benefit.

In September 1991, the Lithuanian government paid parts of some salaries with money vouchers that could be used instead of the ruble, the unstable Soviet currency. Only Lithuanian citizens received the vouchers. Lithuanian leaders hoped this policy would eliminate the **black market** (the informal trading of goods). The vouchers stopped non-Lithuanians from purchasing Lithuanian goods with nearly worthless rubles and then reselling them for large profits on the black market in other republics.

In late 1992, the government issued coupons to replace the ruble, the old Russian currency. Eventually a new Lithuanian currency—the lita—will be used exclusively. Scandinavian bank loans and investments may also help to stabilize Lithuania's newly independent economy.

After independence, Lithuanians showed their disdain for Soviet money and medals by defacing and destroying them.

CHAPTER FOUR

What's Next for Lithuania?

O n May 9, 1990, to celebrate the 45th anniversary of the end of World War II, the Soviet government gave most workers the day off with pay. Many Latvians and Estonians, however, chose to work. They sent their day's wages to Lithuania to aid the republic in its push for self-rule. Estonians and Latvians recognized that Lithuania's success in achieving freedom would be the signal for their own liberation from Soviet occupation.

The Baltic States—which have much in common culturally, historically, and geographically—have already agreed to form an economic alliance. Joining Lithuania's agricultural productivity to the manufacturing capabilities of Latvia and Estonia could bolster the economies of all three countries.

The end of the Soviet system came at a heavy price, however. No longer dependent on Soviet quotas and investment, the Lithuanian economy has struggled on its own. Shortages of costly energy

A farmer in southeastern Lithuania contemplates the country's many challenges, which include modernizing the agricultural sector, revamping the economy, and establishing international trade connections.

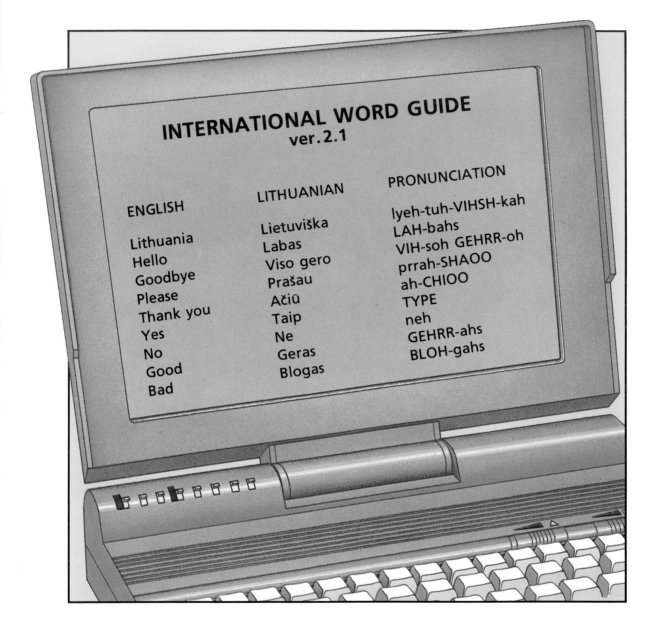

INTERNATIONAL WORD GUIDE
ver. 2.1

ENGLISH	LITHUANIAN	PRONUNCIATION
Lithuania	Lietuviška	lyeh-tuh-VIHSH-kah
Hello	Labas	LAH-bahs
Goodbye	Viso gero	VIH-soh GEHRR-oh
Please	Prašau	prrah-SHAOO
Thank you	Ačiū	ah-CHIOO
Yes	Taip	TYPE
No	Ne	neh
Good	Geras	GEHRR-ahs
Bad	Blogas	BLOH-gahs

supplies—which must be imported at market prices—are causing hardship. Unemployment is serious, and prices are rising.

The problems have turned many Lithuanians against economic reforms. In parliamentary elections held in November 1992, Lithuanian voters elected the Democratic Labor party—the party of

Biblical scholars study scriptures in Vilnius.

Lithuania's ex-Communist leaders—to a majority in the country's parliament.

Nevertheless, Lithuania's independence from the Communist system is clearly recognizable. Lithuania's flag no longer bears the hammer and sickle—famous symbols of Soviet Communism. Nor does the republic's national anthem praise Lenin, the founder of the USSR. Instead, Lithuanians proudly wave their yellow, green, and red flag and loudly sing about ''the land of heroes.''

FAST FACTS ABOUT LITHUANIA

Total Population	3.7 million
Ethnic Mixture	80 percent Lithuanian 9 percent Russian 7 percent Polish 2 percent Belarussian
CAPITAL and Major Cities	VILNIUS Kaunas, Klaipėda
Major Language	Lithuanian
Major Religion	Roman Catholicism
Year of inclusion in USSR	1940
Status	Fully independent, sovereign state; member of United Nations since 1991

amber: a hard, yellowish petrified resin from the sap of pine trees that can be polished and used in jewelry and other ornaments.

annex: to add a country or territory to the domain of another nation by force.

Baltic States: a common term for Estonia, Latvia, and Lithuania, all of which are independent republics that border the Baltic Sea in northern Europe.

black market: an informal system of exchanging goods that operates outside the state-owned distribution network and that usually charges high prices.

collective-farm program: a system of large agricultural estates worked by a group. The workers usually received a portion of the farm's harvest as wages. On a Soviet collective farm, the central government owned the land, buildings, and machinery.

Commonwealth of Independent States: a union of former Soviet republics that was created by the leaders of Russia, Belarus, and Ukraine in December 1991. The commonwealth has no formal constitution and functions as a loose economic and military association.

Communist: a person who supports Communism—an economic system in which the government owns all farmland and the means of producing goods in factories.

concentration camp: a prison camp for people who are thought to be dangerous or opposed to the ruling government.

The policy of glasnost allowed Lithuanians to criticize the Soviet government more openly. To express their dissatisfaction, demonstrators often burned military medals, Soviet passports, and other symbols of Soviet control.

cooperative: a farm, factory, or other enterprise in which the members of a group produce and market their goods and receive a share of the profits.

coup d'état: French words meaning "blow to the state" that refer to a swift, sudden overthrow of a government.

embargo: a government order that forbids the importing and exporting of goods.

ethnic Lithuanian: a person whose ethnic heritage is Baltic and who speaks Lithuanian.

ethnic Russian: a person whose ethnic heritage is Slavic and who speaks Russian.

glasnost: a Russian word meaning "openness" that refers to a Soviet policy of easing restrictions on writing and speech.

industrialize: to build and modernize factories for the purpose of manufacturing a wide variety of consumer goods and machinery.

joint venture: an economic partnership between a locally owned business and a foreign-owned company.

mass deportation: a large-scale, forced movement of people from one place to another.

midnight sun: a midsummer condition during which the sun can be seen very late at night in certain northern areas of the world.

Molotov-Ribbentrop Pact: a political agreement negotiated by Vyacheslav Molotov of the Soviet Union and Joachim von Ribbentrop of Germany. Signed in 1939, the agreement said that the two nations would not attack one another or interfere with one another's military and political activities. A secret part of the pact stated that Germany would give the USSR a free hand in the Baltic region.

These young newlyweds can look forward to new job opportunities and civic freedoms now that years of Soviet occupation have ended.

Order of Teutonic Knights: a German-Christian military organization that attacked the Baltic region in the mid-1300s.

peat: decayed vegetation that has become densely packed down in swamps and bogs. Peat can be cut, dried, and burned as fuel.

perestroika: a policy of economic restructuring introduced in the late 1980s. Under perestroika, the Soviet state allowed small private businesses to form and loosened its control of industry and agriculture.

quota: the government-set amount of factory goods or food that a group is told to produce.

radioactive: giving off energy in the form of particles or rays as a result of the breaking up of atoms.

Russian Empire: a large kingdom ruled by czars that covered present-day Russia as well as areas to the west and south. It existed from roughly the mid-1500s to 1917.

Russify: to make Russian by imposing the Russian language and culture on non-Russian peoples.

Union of Soviet Socialist Republics (USSR): a large nation in eastern Europe and northern Asia that consisted of 15 member-republics. It existed from 1922 to 1991.

United Nations: an international organization formed after World War II whose primary purpose is to promote world peace through discussion and cooperation.

A worker sets out food at a restaurant in Trakai.

• Photo Acknowledgments •

Photographs are used courtesy of: pp. 1, 2, 5, 8, 9 (top and bottom), 10, 13 (left), 15, 16, 17 (top), 19 (right), 20 (left and right), 22, 23 (left and right), 24, 37 (right), 38, 43 (left and right), 47, 48, 51, 54, 55, Jeff Greenberg; pp. 6, 18, 19 (left), 34, 35, 44, TASS / SOVFOTO; pp. 12 (top and bottom), 13 (right), 17 (bottom), Birute Tautvydas; p. 21 (left), SYGMA; p. 21 (right), © Dennis Noonan; pp. 26, 29, Mansell Collection; pp. 27, 32, 33, Lithuanian Research and Studies Center; p. 28 (left), V. Noreika / Balzekus Museum of Lithuanian Culture; p. 28 (top right and bottom right), Museum of History and Ethnography of Lithuania; p. 36, © Vladimir Vyatkin /Lehtikuva Oy / SABA; pp. 37 (left), 42 (top), 52, Rasa Tautvydas; p. 40, NOVOSTI / SOVFOTO; p. 42, © Petri Puromies / Lehtikuva Oy / SABA; p. 46, © Filip Horvat / SABA. Maps and charts: pp. 14–15, 41, J. Michael Roy; pp. 30–31, 45, 50, 51, Laura Westlund.

Covers: (Front and Back) Jeff Greenberg